WHALES

HUMPBACK WHALES

JOHN F. PREVOST

ABDO & Daughters

Published by Abdo & Daughters, 4940 Viking Drive, Suite 622, Edina, Minnesota 55435.

Library bound edition distributed by Rockbottom Books, Pentagon Tower, P.O. Box 36036, Minneapolis, Minnesota 55435.

Printed in the United States.

Cover Photo credit: Peter Arnold, Inc.

Interior Photo credits: Peter Arnold, Inc.

Edited by Bob Italia

Library of Congress Cataloging-in-Publication Data

Prevost, John F.
    The humpback whale / by John F. Prevost.
        p.   cm. — (Whales)
    Includes bibliographical references and index.
        ISBN 1-56239-479-7
    1. Humpback whale—Juvenile literature. [1. Humpback whale. 2. Whales.]
    I. Title. II. Series: Prevost, John F. Whales.
    QL737.C424P742   1995
    599.5'1—dc20   95-12367
                                                                      CIP
                                                                       AC

ABOUT THE AUTHOR

John Prevost is a marine biologist and diver who has been active in conservation and education issues for the past 18 years. Currently he is living inland and remains actively involved in freshwater and marine husbandry, conservation and education projects.

Contents

HUMPBACK WHALES AND FAMILY

Humpback whales are large **mammals** that live in the sea. Like humans, they are **warm blooded** and breathe air. Humpbacks have only a few hairs along their upper jaw. A thick layer of **blubber** under their skin keeps them warm in cold water.

The name "humpback" describes the whales' style of diving, not their shape. When these whales dive they lift their back above the water surface. This makes them appear humpbacked.

Cousins to the humpback whale are the blue whale, fin whale and minke whale. Humpbacks are called **baleen** whales because they have baleen plates instead of teeth.

Humpbacks are warm blooded and breathe air.

SIZE, SHAPE AND COLOR

The largest measured humpback whale was a 62-foot (19-meter) female. Most female humpbacks only reach 49 feet (15 meters). The males are often smaller.

The humpback's body is black except for the white underside. The long, knobby **flippers** are white or black and can bend. There are rows of bumps along the upper jaw. The throat has **creases**. The skin is always covered with **barnacles**.

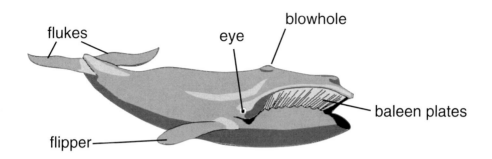

Baleen whales share the same features.

Humpbacks are black except for their undersides which are white.

WHERE THEY LIVE

Humpback whales are found in oceans all around the world. They follow **migration** paths from the **polar** waters to **temperate** waters. **Tropical** waters and the **continents** divide three large groups. Young males, older males, single females, and females with **calves** make up smaller **herds**.

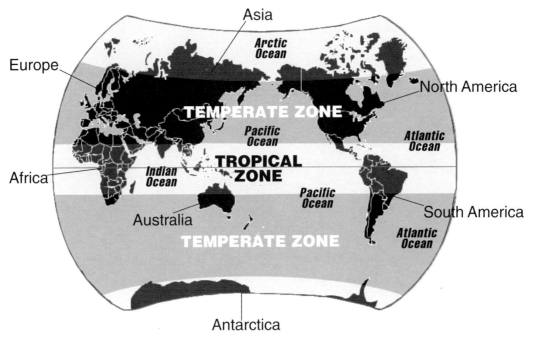

Humpback whales travel in herds from feeding grounds to calving grounds.

The humpbacks travel from feeding grounds to **calving grounds**. They follow the same paths year after year.

SENSES

Humpback whales and people have 4 of the same senses. They can hear better than humans. A humpback whale will sing to other humpbacks through many miles of water. The males will sing to attract mates and warn off rivals. Some songs may last 20 minutes. They also use **echolocation** to find food and avoid enemies.

Their eyesight is good underwater. And they can also see above water by bobbing their head.

HOW ECHOLOCATION WORKS

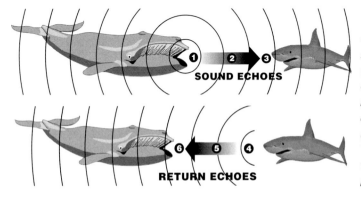

SOUND ECHOES

RETURN ECHOES

The whale sends out sound echoes (1). These echoes travel in all directions through the water (2). The sound echoes reach an object in the whale's path (3), then bounce off it (4). The return echoes travel through the water (5) and reach the whale (6). These echoes let the whale know where the object is, how large it is, and how fast it is moving.

Humpbacks bob out of the water so they can see above the surface.

Touch is an important sense for these **social** animals. They touch each other to show feelings and to **communicate**. Scientists believe humpbacks have the sense of taste. Unlike humans, humpback whales do not have a sense of smell.

DEFENSE

Adult humpback whales have few enemies. Killer whales and large sharks will attack **calves** or weak adults. A humpback whale calf is helpless. It depends on its mother to keep **predators** away.

Swimming away from danger is the humpback's best defense. Although the humpback is a slow whale, it can swim up to 12 miles (19 kilometers) per hour.

In the early 1900s, **whalers** nearly killed all the humpbacks. Now, hunting laws protect them.

The humpback's best defense is swimming from danger.
Humpbacks can swim up to 12 miles (19 km) per hour.

FOOD

Humpback whales do not have teeth. Instead they have **baleen** plates attached to the top of their mouths. The plates bend and are trimmed with bristles.

Humpbacks also have a large throat. It holds water before it is squeezed through the baleen with the whale's tongue. This strains the trapped food from the water. Humpbacks eat **krill**, **plankton**, **anchovy**, and **sardine**.

Humpbacks also trap **prey** inside bubble curtains that they blow from their **blowhole**. The prey will clump in the middle to avoid the bubbles. But then the whale will swim through the trapped prey with its mouth wide open.

Humpback whales have baleen plates instead of teeth. The plates bend and are trimmed with bristles to trap food.

BABIES

Baby whales are called **calves**. At birth, a humpback calf is about 13 feet (4 meters) long. It needs its mother for safety and food.

Since whales are **mammals**, the young calf will **nurse** for up to 10 months. By then the calf is about 26 feet (8 meters) long.

The young whale will not become an adult until it is 8 years old. Males can be 38 feet (11.5 meters) long and females 39 feet (12 meters) long.

*A humpback whale family, including a female
with her calf (far right).*

HUMPBACK WHALE FACTS

Scientific Name: *Megaptera novaengliae*

Average Size: 43 feet (13 meters) - males
45 feet (13.7 meters) - females
62 feet (19 meters) largest measured, a female

Where They're Found: In all oceans but follow seasonal **migration** patterns between the **polar** and **temperate** waters. There are three different groups: North Atlantic, North Pacific, and Southern Hemisphere.

The humpback whale.

GLOSSARY

ANCHOVY (an-CHOE-vee) - Small silvery fish, often less than 10 inches (25.4 cm) long. There are over 100 species.

BALEEN (buh-LEEN) - A hard flexible material growing in place of teeth and attached to the upper jaw; also called whalebone.

BARNACLE (BAR-na-kull) - A crustacean (relative of the crab, lobster and shrimp) having a shell which attaches to shipbottoms, pilings, and whales.

BLOWHOLE - A nostril (or nostrils) found on the top of the head of a whale.

BLUBBER - A thick fatty layer found under the skin of many sea mammals.

CALF - A baby whale.

CALVING GROUNDS - An area where whales will go to safely bear their young.

COMMUNICATION (kuh-mew-nih-KAY-shun) - To exchange or share feelings, thoughts, or information.

CONTINENT - One of the 7 main land masses: Europe, Asia, Africa, North America, South America, Australia and Antarctica.

CREASES - Wrinkles or grooves that allow the throat of a whale to expand and hold water before it is filtered through the baleen.

ECHOLOCATION (ek-oh-low-KAY-shun) - The use of sound waves to find objects.

FLIPPERS - The forelimbs of a sea mammal.

HERD - A group of animals traveling or staying together.

KRILL - A small shrimp-like shellfish found in open water.

MAMMAL - A class of animals, including humans, that have hair and feed their young milk.

MIGRATION (my-GRAY-shun) - To travel periodically from one region to another in search of food or to reproduce.

NURSE - To feed a young animal or child milk from the mother's breasts.

PLANKTON - A group of floating or drifting plants and animals, often at or near the surface of the water.

POLAR - Either the Arctic (north pole) or Antarctic (south pole) regions.

PREDATOR (PRED-uh-tor) - An animal that eats other animals.

PREY - Animals that are eaten by other animals.

SARDINE - Small herring-like fish, often less than 16 inches (.5 meters) in length.

SOCIAL (SOW-shull) - Living in organized groups.

TEMPERATE (TEM-prit) - The part of the Earth where the oceans are not very hot, or not very cold.

TROPICAL (TRAH-pih-kull) - The part of the Earth near the equator where the oceans are very warm.

WARM-BLOODED - An animal whose body temperature remains the same and warmer than the outside air or water temperature.

WHALER - A person involved in the hunting and processing of whales.

Index

BIBLIOGRAPHY

Cousteau, Jacques-Yves. *The Whale, Mighty Monarch of the Sea.* N.Y.: Doubleday, 1972.

Dozier, Thomas A. *Whales and Other Sea Mammals.* Time-Life Films, 1977.

Leatherwood, Stephen. *The Sierra Club Handbook of Whales and Dolphins.* San Francisco, California: Sierra Club Books, 1983.

Minasian, Stanley M. *The World's Whales.* Washington, D.C.: Smithsonian Books, 1984.

Ridgway, Sam H., ed. *Mammals of the Sea.* Springfield, Illinois: Charles C. Thomas Publisher, 1972.